EARTH VERSE

Explore our Planet through Poetry and Art

For Hannah Mahoney, haiku poet and copy-editor extraordinaire,
and for those who, late at night, count syllables instead of sheep
S.M.W.

For Mark Brimble — a force of nature
W.G.

First published 2018 by Walker Studio,
an imprint of Walker Books Ltd, 87 Vauxhall Walk, London SE11 5HJ

2 4 6 8 10 9 7 5 3 1

Text © 2018 Sally M. Walker

Illustrations © 2018 William Grill

The right of Sally M. Walker and William Grill to be identified as author and illustrator
respectively of this work has been asserted by them in accordance with the Copyright,
Designs and Patents Act 1988

This book has been typeset in Intro Book and Dante Regular

Printed in China

British Library Cataloguing in Publication Data: a catalogue record for this book is available
from the British Library

ISBN 978-1-4063-7649-4

www.walkerstudio.com

EARTH VERSE

Explore our Planet through Poetry and Art

SALLY M. WALKER

illustrated by **WILLIAM GRILL**

WALKER STUDIO

AN IMPRINT OF WALKER BOOKS

third one from the sun,
Earth's blue and white majesty
dwarfs her lunar child

fragile outer crust,
shell around mantle and core —
Earth: a hard-boiled egg

gold, silver, copper,
sapphires, rubies, emeralds –
glittery Earth-bling

cleaved into thin sheets,
mica's panes invite sunlight —
natural window

molten magma stew
bubbles out of its hot pot,
chills into hard rock

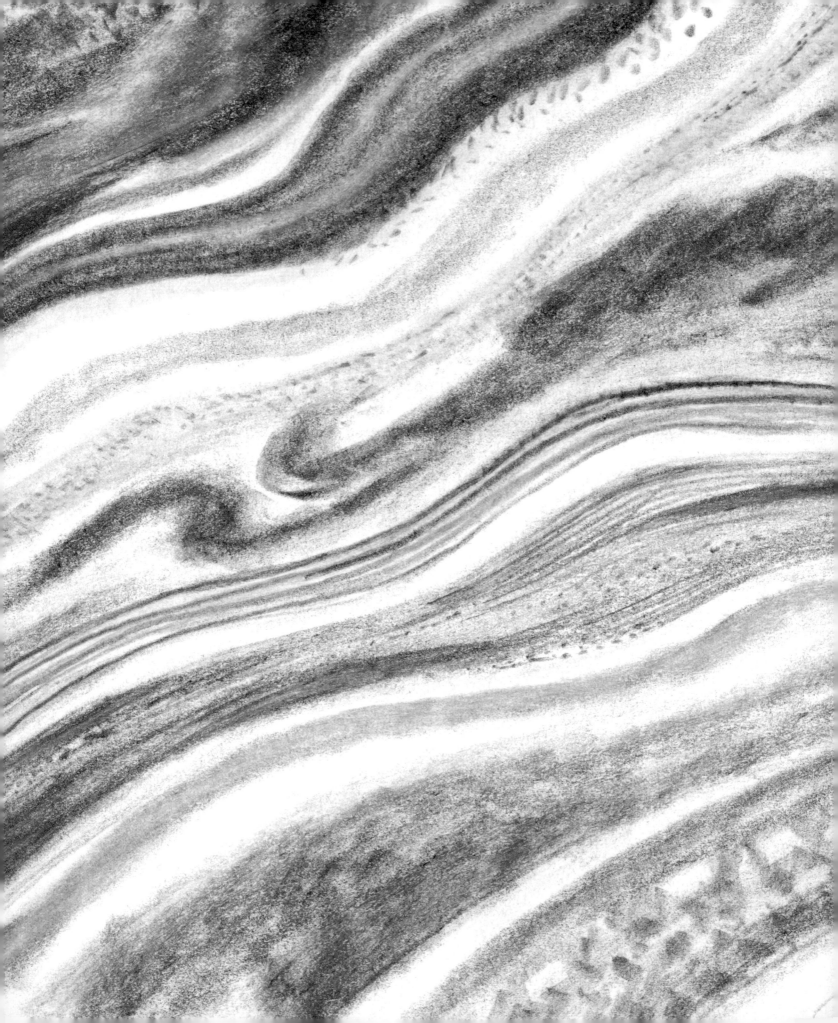

layered sediments
stuck tight with mineral glue
build layered Earth-stripes

check out a new look:
metamorphic makeover
turns granite to gneiss

unscalable cliff —
canyon's stone-faced guardian
forever on watch

silica, ghost-like,
drifts into wood and shouts, "Boo!" —
petrified forest

nestled in sandstone,
Maiasaura shields her young
fossil family

energy unleashed
shoots waves through the brittle crust —
trees topple down cliffs

seafloor tug-of-war:
a tsunami drowns the shore,
neighbourhoods vanish

hot-headed mountain
loses its cool, spews ash cloud —
igneous tantrum

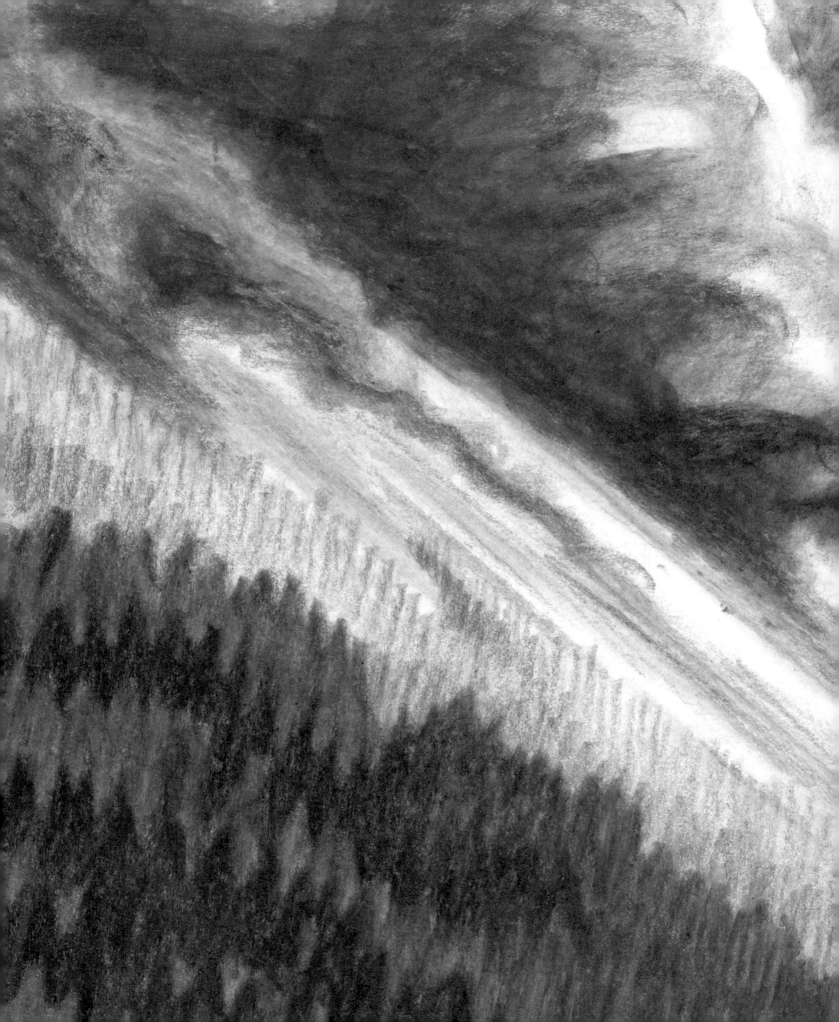

pyroclastic flow
rushes down Vesuvius ...
a ghost dog lingers

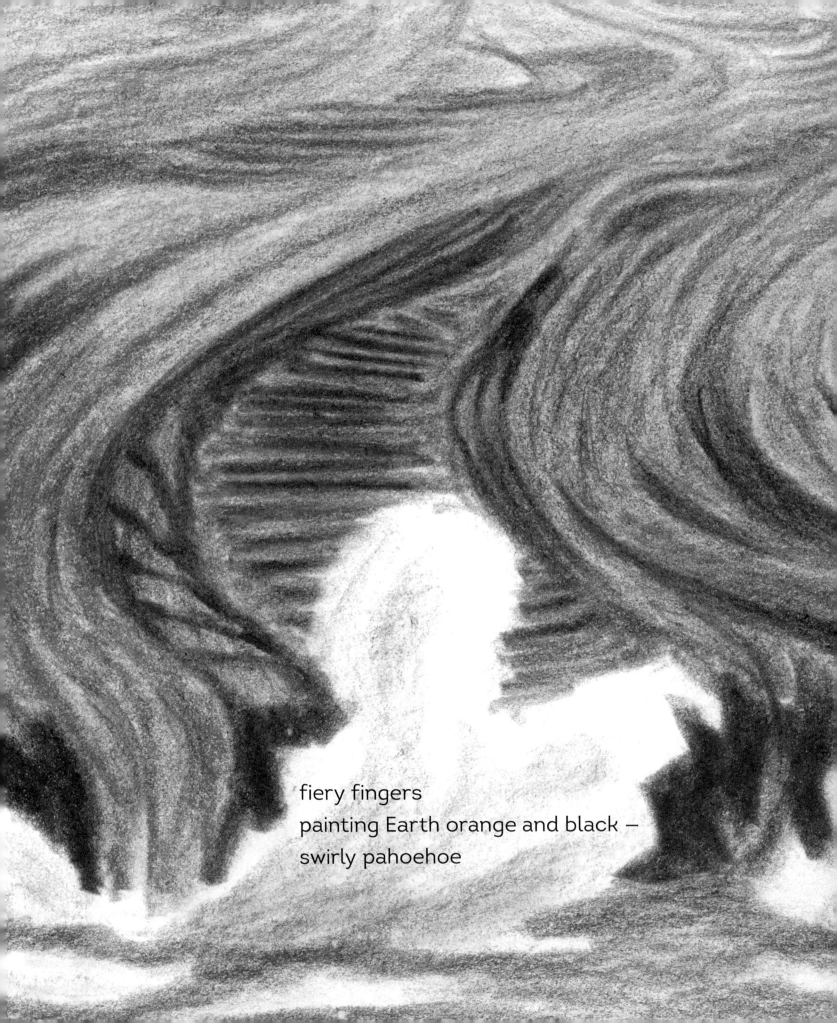

fiery fingers
painting Earth orange and black —
swirly pahoehoe

hot rock meets cold sea,
shatters lava to black sand ...
a crab tiptoes home

sky shenanigans:
lightning bullies storm clouds with
thunderous results

birds sleep in their nests
winds unfurl a fog blanket ...
leaves sing lullabies

mountain stream rushes,
ancient river meanders –
hare and tortoise race

a flat stone, skipping,
casts circles across the lake,
lassoing the fish

sediment-filled waves
tumble in a frothy foam ...
a gull wears sand socks

no bucket needed,
the sea builds its own castle ...
flowers bloom on dunes

deep layers of ice:
a continent-size blanket —
Earth's crust mattress sags

relentless glaciers
pluck and smooth steep valley walls,
changing V to U

ready for the plunge,
ice slides off rocky playgrounds
and calves with a splash

titanic iceberg
buoyantly cruises the deep —
ship, keep your distance!

underground water
trickles through a sandstone sponge,
pools inside the well

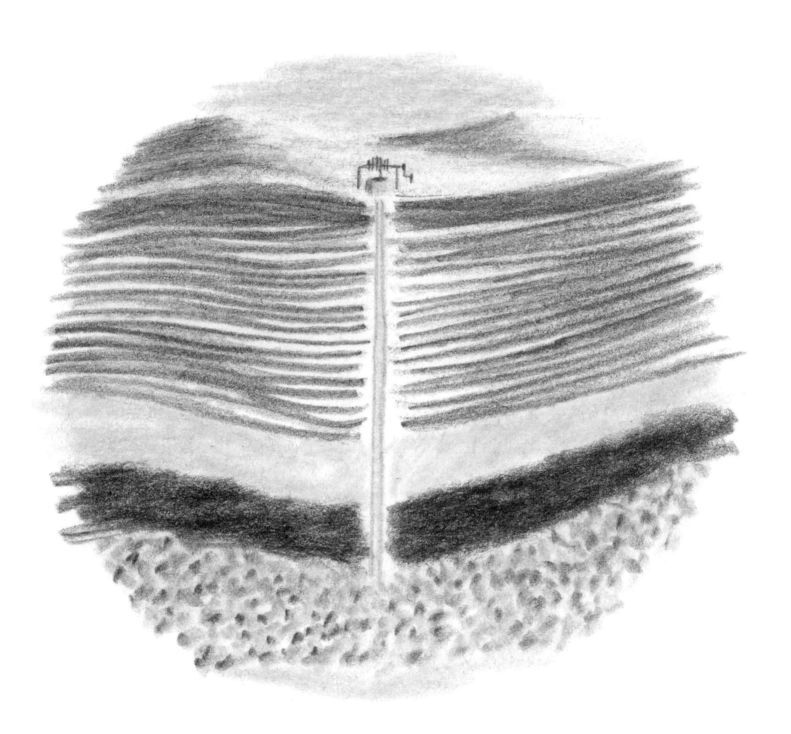

hold fast, stalactite,
everlasting icicle,
stone bed for a bat

stalagmite! reach high!
catch the ceiling's drip, drip, drip,
grow up from the ground

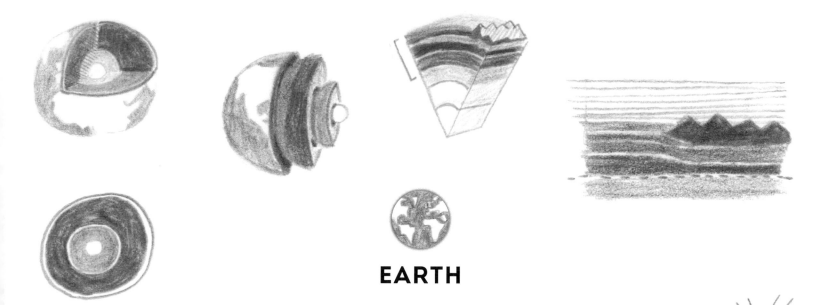

EARTH

In some ways, Earth is rather like a hard-boiled egg. The crust, Earth's outer layer, is a brittle shell that can easily crack and shatter under pressure. The mantle, Earth's thick middle layer, bends like the white part of the hard-boiled egg. It's made of hot, squeezable rock that oozes and flows without breaking. Earth's centre, or core, is made up of two parts: a solid inner core surrounded by a liquid outer core. The temperature where the two parts touch each other is as hot as the surface of the sun.

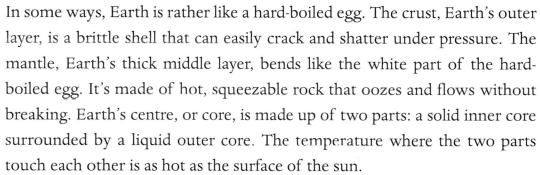

Earth's moon was an accident, the result of a humongous crash. Scientists believe that Earth was hit by a celestial body about half its size. The fiery impact threw tons of Earth's crust and mantle into space. Earth's gravitational pull kept the mantle debris orbiting Earth like a cosmic hula hoop. Over tens of thousands of years, the orbiting debris combined and formed the moon.

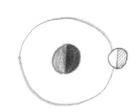

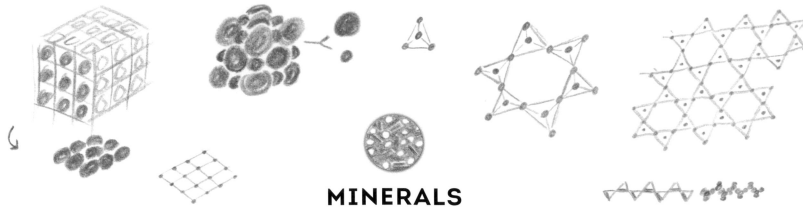

MINERALS

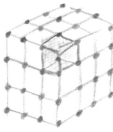

Minerals are solid, non-living substances found in nature. Each mineral has its own special arrangement of atoms. Those arrangements create many interesting shapes. Some minerals are long, pointy crystals. Others are shaped like cubes. Some look like heaps of soap bubbles. The way a mineral's atoms are arranged means that when the mineral breaks, it does so in certain ways. The mineral mica breaks apart into sheets that are almost paper-thin.

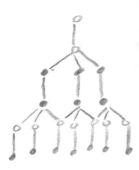

Depending on its chemical ingredients, a mineral can be any colour found in the rainbow. Minerals can be hard or soft. Diamonds, rubies and sapphires are hard enough to scratch glass. Yet people can powder their skin with talc, a mineral so soft your fingernail can scratch it. The mineral quartz is made of a chemical compound called silica. Most seashore sand grains are quartz. Silica is one of the main ingredients used to make glass.

Our homes would be stark, boring places without minerals. Paint, floor tiles and screws all contain minerals, as do roads and pavements. And pencils write with the mineral graphite.

ROCKS

Rocks form when minerals crystallize (solidify) or when natural processes cement pieces of minerals and broken rock together. Earth's three main groups of rock are known as igneous, sedimentary and metamorphic.

Igneous rocks begin as magma. Born in the mantle, magma is toothpaste-thick, fiery-hot melted rock. It oozes upwards into the crust or onto Earth's surface, where it cools into a solid igneous rock. Many roads are built on top of a bed of crushed basalt, an abundantly found igneous rock.

Tiny pieces of broken rock are called sediments. Broken shells and bone are sediments too. Water, wind and ice sweep sediments from one place to another. They deposit them in accumulating layers that can be thousands of feet thick. Sometimes the weight of the top layers squeezes the sediments in the lower layers so tightly together that they become hard rock. Other times, water containing dissolved minerals seeps into loose sediments. When the dissolved minerals crystallize, they glue the sediments together. Rock formed from hardened or cemented sediments is called sedimentary rock. Sandstone, frequently used as a building stone, is a sedimentary rock.

Heat and pressure change a rock's texture and structure. They force a rock's minerals to rearrange themselves in new patterns. Some of the minerals may chemically change into a different mineral. A rock that has been changed by heat and pressure is called a metamorphic rock. Under heat and pressure, the sedimentary rock called limestone becomes the metamorphic rock called marble. Artists sculpt statues in marble. The igneous rock called granite becomes gneiss.

FOSSILS

Giant bones or razor-sharp teeth may be all that's left of lumbering dinosaurs and sharks longer than a school bus, but their hardened remains, called fossils, can teach us a lot about ancient life forms. But fossils are much more than just bones and teeth. Skin, eggs, nests, footprints and even a worm's trail can be fossils. The leaves, flowers and stems of a plant can become a fossil too. When any of these items is naturally preserved, its fossil is like a stone photograph of ancient life forms and the environments they lived in.

Most fossils are found in sedimentary rock. That's because the remains were buried by sediments, which protected them from destruction. The remains later hardened into rock along with the sediment. But naturally occurring chemicals dissolved in water can also seep into the pores of bones and wood. Inside the pores, the chemicals combine and form a mineral. When the mineral crystallizes, the bone or piece of wood turns into stone. The fossilized tree trunks found in Petrified Forest National Park, in Arizona, formed this way.

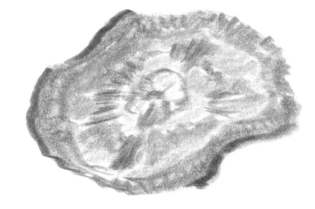

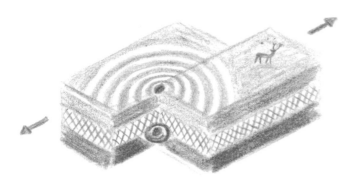

EARTHQUAKES

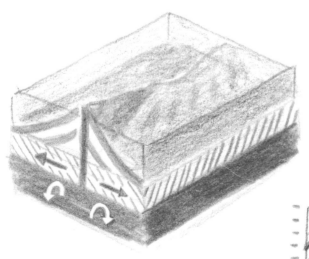

Forces inside Earth squeeze and stretch the rock that makes up its brittle crust. When forces push or pull the rock too much, it cracks. But they still keep squeezing and stretching. That causes energy to build up inside the cracked rock. Sometimes the energy becomes more than the rock can bear. Suddenly, the rock on one side of the crack jerks loose from the rock on the other side. Waves of energy ripple away from the crack, now called a fault. The travelling waves make the rock vibrate and quake. Earthquakes damage buildings and roads and can cause landslides. Earthquakes beneath an ocean can trigger a water wave called a tsunami. By the time a tsunami reaches land, it can be 50 to 100 feet tall. A tsunami's power can wipe out everything in its path.

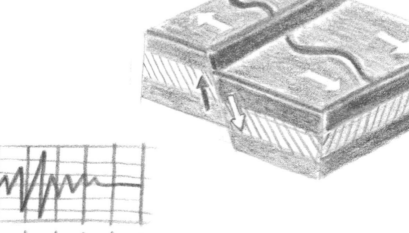

VOLCANOES

A volcano can be a towering mountain, a small hill, an enormous crater or a crack on the ocean floor. A volcano forms whenever magma erupts onto Earth's surface. When magma reaches the surface, it is called lava. Lava can have very different appearances. The surface of pahoehoe lava is smooth and ropy, while another kind of lava, called aa, is rough and sharp.

Volcanoes spew steamy clouds that contain fragments of magma and rock called pyroclasts. Sometimes a cloud of boiling hot pyroclasts collapses and rushes down a volcano's flanks. Travelling at speeds up to hundreds of miles per hour, a pyroclastic flow destroys everything in its path. The pyroclastic flow that occurred after Mount Vesuvius erupted in AD 79 killed nearly 16,000 people and buried the towns of Pompeii and Herculaneum. It buried animals as well – even a dog. The pyroclasts hardened and became a stone mould around the bodies. Casts made from these moulds become ghostly reminders of lost lives.

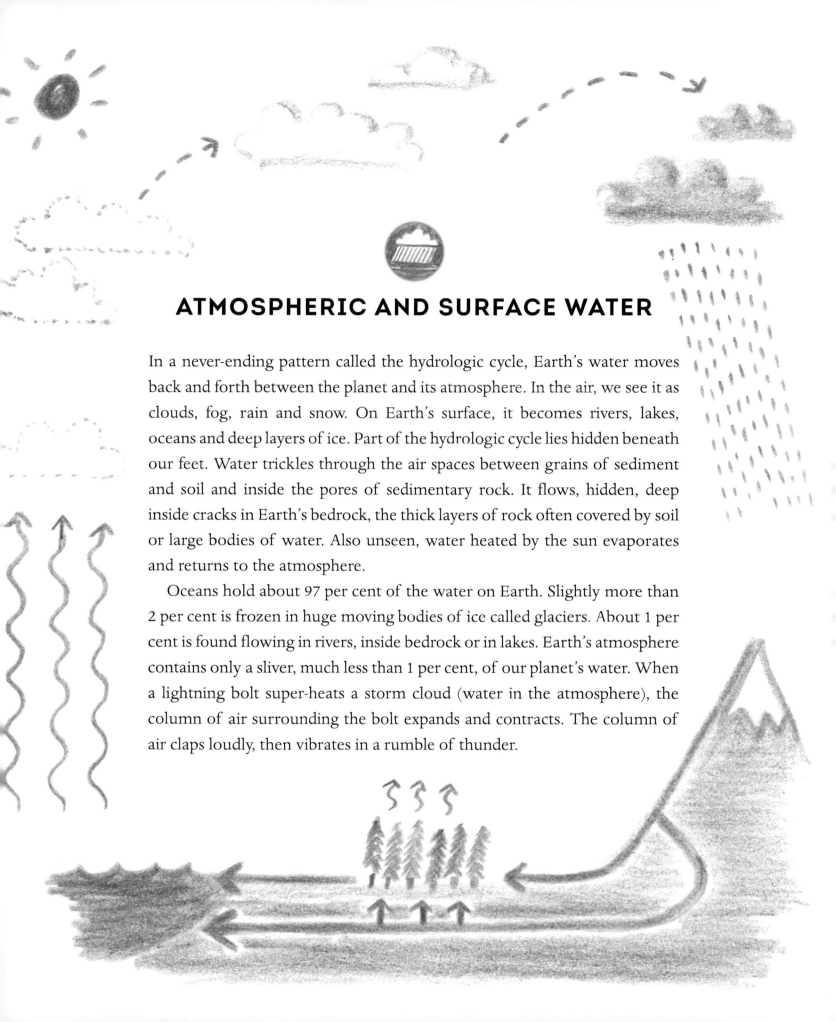

ATMOSPHERIC AND SURFACE WATER

In a never-ending pattern called the hydrologic cycle, Earth's water moves back and forth between the planet and its atmosphere. In the air, we see it as clouds, fog, rain and snow. On Earth's surface, it becomes rivers, lakes, oceans and deep layers of ice. Part of the hydrologic cycle lies hidden beneath our feet. Water trickles through the air spaces between grains of sediment and soil and inside the pores of sedimentary rock. It flows, hidden, deep inside cracks in Earth's bedrock, the thick layers of rock often covered by soil or large bodies of water. Also unseen, water heated by the sun evaporates and returns to the atmosphere.

Oceans hold about 97 per cent of the water on Earth. Slightly more than 2 per cent is frozen in huge moving bodies of ice called glaciers. About 1 per cent is found flowing in rivers, inside bedrock or in lakes. Earth's atmosphere contains only a sliver, much less than 1 per cent, of our planet's water. When a lightning bolt super-heats a storm cloud (water in the atmosphere), the column of air surrounding the bolt expands and contracts. The column of air claps loudly, then vibrates in a rumble of thunder.

GLACIERS

In very cold places, some snowflakes never completely melt. Instead, they become rounded, icy grains that accumulate in layers from year to year. Up to 100 years may pass before the weight of the layers squeezes all the air from the tiny spaces between the grains. When almost all the air is gone, the icy grains become glacial ice.

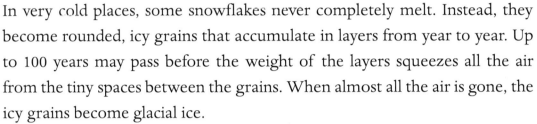

Glacial ice fills bowl-shaped hollows near mountain tops. In frigid Antarctica, miles-deep ice sheets blanket most of the continent. No matter where thick ice layers form, the upper layers press hard enough on the ice below to make the lower layers bend. The ice starts moving the way a ball of soft clay moves when it is pressed flat. And it will keep flowing, even across flat land. Once a huge mass of ice starts flowing, it is called a glacier. Gigantic glaciers are so heavy that Earth's crust sags beneath their weight.

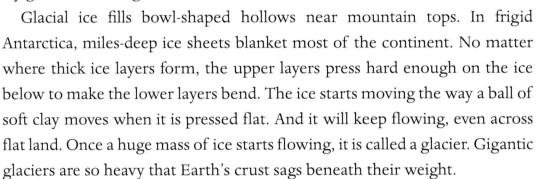

Glaciers have tremendous power. A glacier that flows into a V-shaped mountain valley plucks rock from its walls, scouring them into a broad U-shaped valley. Glaciers often carry gigantic boulders from one place to another. When a glacier shoves into the sea, huge chunks of ice calve, or break off, from the glacier's edge and float away as icebergs. In 1912, if the *Titanic* hadn't encountered an iceberg, it probably would have arrived safely in New York City.

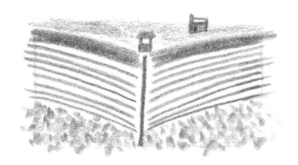

GROUNDWATER

Beneath Earth's surface, water travels through bedrock in the tiny air spaces between the rock's mineral and sediment grains. When people drill a well, it fills with this water, which is called groundwater.

Most caves form when groundwater trickles inside cracks found in bedrock (a thick layer of buried rock) that is made of limestone, a sedimentary rock. Acids found naturally in groundwater slowly dissolve the bedrock, enlarging the cracks and creating a large open space. A cave can be a single chamber, or a vast network of connecting chambers. Groundwater filled with dissolved minerals drips, slips and puddles inside caves. The minerals crystallize and create the icicle-like stone formations called stalactites and stalagmites. One way to remember which is which is that stalactites (with a *c*) *cling* to the *ceiling,* while stalagmites (with a *g*) *grow* from the *ground*. Sometimes a stalactite grows so long that it connects with a stalagmite. Together, they form a column.

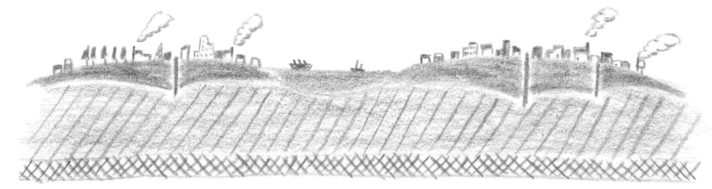

SUGGESTIONS FOR FURTHER READING

Branley, Franklyn M. *Volcanoes.* Illustrated by Megan Lloyd. New York: HarperCollins, 2008.

Hooper, Meredith. *The Drop in My Drink: The Story of Water on Our Planet.* Illustrated by Chris Coady. London: Frances Lincoln Children's Books, 2015.

Patent, Dorothy Hinshaw. *Shaping the Earth.* Photographs by William Muñoz. New York: Clarion, 2000.

Prager, Ellen J. *Earthquakes.* Illustrated by Susan Greenman. Washington, DC: National Geographic, 2002.

Rusch, Elizabeth. *Eruption! Volcanoes and the Science of Saving Lives.* Photographs by Tom Uhlman. Boston: Houghton Mifflin Harcourt, 2013.

Simon, Seymour. *Oceans.* London: Harper Collins, 2006.

Walker, Sally M. *Figuring Out Fossils.* Minneapolis: Lerner, 2013.

———. *Glaciers.* Minneapolis: Lerner, 2008.

———. *Marveling at Minerals.* Minneapolis: Lerner, 2013.

———. *Researching Rocks.* Minneapolis: Lerner, 2013.

Wells, Robert E. *Did a Dinosaur Drink This Water?* Morton Grove, IL: Albert Whitman, 2006.